Red Squirrel's adventure

Story by Beverley Randell

Illustrations by Isabel Lowe

Red Squirrel looked down
from her home in the trees.
She was hungry.

She saw some nuts
over in the grass.
She ran down the tree
and raced across the ground
to get one.

But a big gray bird
was flying around
over the trees.
He was looking for food,
and he liked to eat squirrels.

The gray bird
saw Red Squirrel,
down on the ground.

Red Squirrel did not see
the gray bird.
She was eating a nut,
and she was not looking
up at the sky.

The gray bird flew down
very fast.

He was going
to catch Red Squirrel
with his big claws.

Red Squirrel looked up.

She started to run,

but it was too late

to get back to the trees.

She had nowhere to hide.

The big bird

got her by the tail.

The big gray bird flew
up into the sky
with Red Squirrel.

But then an eagle saw them
and came flying down!

The eagle liked
to eat squirrels, too.

The eagle wanted
to take Red Squirrel away
from the gray bird.

The two birds started to fight.

The gray bird let go
of Red Squirrel's tail.
Down she fell!

The birds came flying down

after Red Squirrel,

but by then

she was safe in the treetops.

Red Squirrel was so pleased
to be home again!

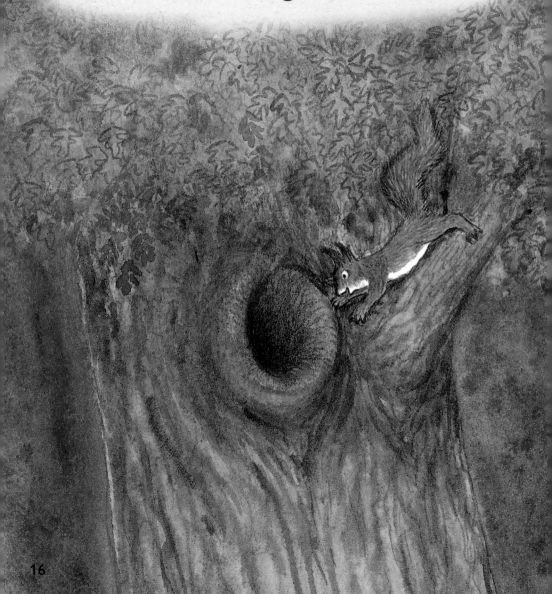